THE FIRST

SHALL BE LAST

TRANSFORMATIONAL LEADERSHIP

BOBI KRUEMBERG

CONTENTS

Dedication

I dedicate this book to my son, Rett Kruemberg, with my prayer for you being, to lead like the king. Never forget whose child you are! You are God's child, and He has created you for a purpose beyond your imagination. Fight for it! With everything in your power, aggressively seek out His path. Keep pushing forward. Never give up. Work hard. Try new things, and trust God to do the rest. I am so proud He chose me to be your mother.

With special thanks to all of the leaders who have served as my inspiration in so many different ways: Julie Stein, Mike West, Michael Genot, Sue Baron, Dusty Rhodes, Bill Hobbs, Susan Hess, Michelle Montanez, Shannon Rochester, Jennifer Bargo, Maureen Gomes, Arianna Atehortua, Marc Vorkapich, and Joanie Williams.

I am incredibly thankful to my cheerleaders who helped me see this project through to completion: Stefanie Braswell, for your amazing editing and advice; Mike Marlow and Stacey Jo Coffee-Thorn, for your timely words of affirmation.

Randy Lundi, thank you for believing in me and giving me the space to work it out on my own. Thank you for loving me and demonstrating your leadership as a man of God.

To my biggest fan and loudest cheerleader, Julia Apotheker—you have been my mentor my entire life, and I pray that I can be the servant leader you have always been. Thank you for giving me a role model of being the hands and feet of Jesus.

Acknowledgment

I am deeply thankful for the breathtaking artwork of the late West Coast "Illuminism" artist Leszek Forczek, who unexpectedly crossed the "rainbow threshold" May 20, 2019, at the age of 72. Forczek's paintings are characterized by their unique sense of luminosity, space, and movement, harmonizing the inner and outer aspects of Light, Color, and Darkness: this balance of inner and outer is, in its essence, beauty, art, and life. A very special acknowledgement is due to his beautiful wife, Casse Forczek, for providing me Forczek's artwork to share with you.

The front cover: "Washing of the Feet"

I chose this piece of art to demonstrate the beauty of crafting your leadership style after the greatest Leader that has ever walked our planet. There is great satisfaction in embracing true service as your purpose in this world. In fact, it is the key to unlocking the beauty of your position, your people, and the world around us.

About the Author

Bobi grew up in the snowbelt of northeastern Pennsylvania. She graduated from Keystone College with a degree in Communications. Soon out of college, she grew tired of the cold and made her home in Florida. Bobi approaches leadership with an incredibly diverse background. She started her career in TV broadcasting and theatre production while simultaneously managing restaurants to pay the bills. When she first moved to Florida, she joined a large "mega" church and began leading the drama ministry and writing original scripts for the services. Experiencing church leadership is the ember that sparked Bobi's yearning to become a different type of leader. As she witnessed systems being promoted over people, Bobi believed the system was broken.

Early on in her career, she began to branch out into many different avenues with a strong motivation to contribute to the betterment of something bigger than herself. Bobi was a successful fundraiser for several nonprofit organizations, in addition to working as an advertising executive for a Christian radio station. She was a worship arts director on the pastoral staff for a second church while serving on an architectural team in charge of building a community center. Bobi has dedicated the past 26 years working in Christian radio as an on-air talent as well as fundraising.

It was 16 years ago when Bobi discovered a new purpose, working in senior living and health care. She has embodied the motto of "Leading by Example" as a Senior Executive Director. Bobi has taken all the knowledge from secular and Christian business to compose this Bible study that is relatable and instructional to all sectors.

Outside of work, Bobi has a 22-year-old son. They enjoy fishing, traveling, snorkeling, and hitting the gym together. In her volunteer work, Bobi serves as the

Fund Raising Chair for Southeast Florida Honor Flight, an organization serving our wartime veterans, and Florida Faith Alliance, bringing attention and healing to human trafficking victims.

"Jesus did not come into this world to *be* served. He came into the world *to* serve…."

Mathew 20:28

Preface

"Trust in the Lord with all your heart and lean not on your own understanding."

What? I thought I was picking up a leadership book... "Lean not on my own understanding"? What am I supposed to do with that statement? I get paid for my understanding! People expect me to understand. Unless I'm a pastor (and even then), "I lean on the Lord" doesn't really look great on a résumé.

"In all your ways acknowledge him and He will direct your path."
Proverbs 3:6

Great. Thanks again, but I don't work in a Christian business. I actually have to lead people to do their jobs. I have to manage people, and I am expected to produce results. I can't just say, "Praise the Lord" all day!

I get it. I don't work in a Christian ministry today. I'm an Executive Director in the healthcare industry. I used to work in ministry. I have spent over 20 years in Christian radio as a DJ and as a fundraiser for local ministries and Christian radio stations. I was on the pastoral staff of a church during a couple of chapters of my journey, and prior to that, I worked in the restaurant industry.

I've had the opportunity to follow some great leaders. But I've also had a lot of mediocre—and even abysmal—leaders whom I had to attempt to follow. But it was through the toughest roads, under the worst leadership, that I learned the most. In those moments, I learned the best lesson in leadership: I learned about the leader I did not want to become.

In this devotional, I'll be sharing with you what God has taught me about leadership in a format that's easy to read and apply. I like books that are quick to read and have concrete applications. So I won't dawdle in flowery idealism and unproductive scenarios. I promise to respect your time—because if you picked up a leadership book, I know you're busy! My objective is to give you some behavior-changing, paradigm-shifting lessons that will transform your business as you create a Christ-centered culture in a secular environment.

And by no means am I excluding those in ministry or Christian leadership. If you work in Christian ministry, hopefully these principles aren't foreign to you. But maybe you're not witnessing servant leadership in action. In my many years of "kingdom work," as they called it, I saw very little servant leadership. And I wish I had known then what I know now.

Lastly, if you think you know how to lead and have been doing it for a while, yet you still picked up this book, I ask you now: Will you take this time to trust that God may have something new for you, and that He may want to change your understanding?

My hope for you is that your heart will be inspired. That you'll be excited to lead in a new way, creating an authentic culture where people are valued and thrive. Once we are able to achieve that culture, our organizations will expand beyond our expectations. I pray God will show Himself to you and give you a fresh perspective into His purpose for your life. We are all a part of Christ's body, but we all have a different purpose in His body. We are His hands, feet, and voice in this world. Therefore, our responsibility is to strive for peace and understanding as we serve each other in order to show the world His love.

You are exactly where He wants you to be today!

Introduction

What is a Servant Leader?

The word *leader* is defined as "the person who commands a group or organization," according to Webster's.

The same dictionary defines the word *servant* as "someone who performs duties for others" or a "devoted and helpful follower or supporter."

Piecing these together, then, a servant leader is a person who commands a group by being supportive and devoted to helping it perform its duties.

This is the simplest definition of a servant leader I could think of, but the application of this management style can be far more complex. That's because, for many, it requires a paradigm shift in the way we think of leadership. If you want to grow in this area, it requires a level of personal involvement that may stretch you outside of your comfort zone. It may require you to remove some barriers you've placed around yourself. Being a true servant leader requires you to get your hands dirty daily.

But *why* servant leadership?

There's an expression that has been my professional mantra for decades: *"Speed of the leader, speed of the team."* I challenge you to adopt this mantra as your own.

When a leader sets the tone and pace for their people and leads them by example, the team will either naturally model that same tone and pace, or members will weed themselves out of the organization. Leading by example, therefore, is the fundamental building block to changing organizational culture.

I'm not sure it was Gandhi or Michael Jackson who said it, but it's worth repeating: *"Be the change you want to see."* As a servant leader, you have the power to change lives by valuing people, building authentic relationships, and pouring your energies into your team. You can dramatically change the culture of your business or organization by modeling the behaviors of a servant leader outlined in the next chapters.

Okay then, *how* do you become a servant leader?

We find the greatest-ever example of servant leadership in the man who led a revolution and changed the trajectory of the entire world. You don't need to be a Christian to understand the powerful impact Jesus had on history and his impact on human relationships. Thankfully, in the Bible, we have a playbook to follow so we can model our lives and our leadership style after His.

You can read the story of His life in the New Testament to find hundreds of examples of His transformative servant leadership, and by modeling His behaviors, you can dramatically change the culture of your business or organization. I'll outline some of His key servant leader behaviors in the next chapters, but I believe the greatest picture we have of true servant leadership happened the night before Jesus was crucified.

A couple thousand years ago, Jesus and His twelve closest friends had been walking the dirty, dusty streets of Roman-occupied Jerusalem in nothing but strappy leather sandals. As you can imagine, those streets were covered in trash, decaying food, and not only animal excrement; since this was long before modern-day plumbing, human excrement was very common.

When the thirteen men arrived at the home where they would be having dinner, they expected to have their feet washed by one of the servants of the household. And not just any servant—the lowest-ranking servant would've been the one tasked with cleaning the soles of the guests. This servant may not have had any visible talent or skill and was therefore relegated to the most menial of tasks. The master of the house or his guests likely wouldn't have shown this servant much respect, if they paid him any attention at all. I imagine such a servant would've felt invisible.

On this night, however, he was relieved of his dirty duty.

When Jesus and His friends arrived, likely tired from the heat and from travel, Jesus decided to demonstrate servant leadership in the most unusual, yet tangible, way. He grabbed the bowl of water and the towel reserved for the dirtiest of tasks. He knelt down on His knees and began to wash His friends' feet.

Not long before this moment, Jesus had been teaching crowds of thousands. At this point in His ministry, people routinely flocked to Him, adoring Him as they hung on His every word. Yet here, on that floor, knelt Jesus. He humbled Himself, washing the feet of His companions one after another. As He wiped the filth from their toes, He showed them how to serve each other and mankind.

What's more, Jesus knew that Judas had betrayed Him. He knew Judas had already gone to the Jewish officials and was paid handsomely to turn Jesus in to be arrested. Jesus knew the armed guards would be coming for Him later that night. Yet, when the time came to wash Judas' feet, Jesus didn't flinch. He didn't pass him by. He washed the feet of the friend who betrayed Him with the same care and compassion as He had shown His other devoted followers. He dried Judas' feet with the tenderness He showed the other eleven men.

I'm certain these twelve men were shocked, confused, and even felt awkward. We see in John 13 that some of the men wanted to refuse His service. So Jesus explained His actions. He said:

"Do you understand what I have done for you? You call me 'Teacher' or 'Lord' and rightly so, for that is what I am. Now that I, your Lord and Teacher, have washed your feet you should also wash one another's. I have set you an example. Very truly I tell you, no servant is greater than his master and no messenger is greater than the one who sent him. Now that you know these things, you will be blessed if you do them."

Whose feet are you washing today?

Leadership is exemplified in servanthood. Servant leadership is not just a management style. It is a lifestyle! Jesus told us that *"Whatever we do for the least of these,"* we are doing for Him. It means never saying "Me first," but instead choosing to put others before yourself. Whether you're holding the door for the person behind you, giving up the front parking spot, or cleaning the public restroom even though you didn't make the mess, you are serving the Lord. Be determined to leave every place better than you found it.

Paul told us in Colossians 3:23, **"Whatever you do, work at it with all your heart as if you are working for the Lord, not for humans."** Jesus also told us, **"The greatest among you will be your servant."** I used to think that scripture meant God was going to one day promote a janitor to CEO as His way of being clever—and He very well may! But as I've grown, I think what Jesus meant was that the person who serves is already the greatest in the Lord's eyes.

So, the first step to becoming a servant leader is to agree with this statement and to make it your prayer:

"Lord, I want to serve others, as a way of serving You, in the place where You have placed me."

Repeat those words and let God open your eyes to the unique position where He has purposefully placed you. Now, let Him give you a vision for that service.

"Whoever is first will be last and whoever is last shall be first."

Matthew 19:30

In what way are you willing to serve someone today?

_____

_____

_____

_____

_____

_____

_____

Does this idea of becoming a servant leader in a tangible way make you uncomfortable? Why or why not?

_____

_____

_____

_____

_____

_____

_____

Does it seem possible in your business or organization?

_____

_____

_____

_____

_____

_____

_____

_____

_____

What will be the most difficult change?

_____

_____

_____

_____

_____

_____

_____

What culture shift do you want to see in your own life or in the life of your business?

_____

_____

_____

_____

_____

_____

_____

Write out an honest prayer asking God to shine His light of truth on your heart and in your mind to become the leader He wants you to be in this season of life.

_____

_____

_____

_____

_____

_____

_____

_____

PART ONE

Inspect What You Expect of Yourself

[Leaders] need to be worthy of all honor so that God is honored.

1 Timothy 6:1 (Paraphrased)

Becoming a true servant leader begins with **awareness**—not only of your actions, but also of your intentions. Sometimes, figuring out your own intentions and motivators can feel like peeling an onion. It can make your eyes water, and you may find your personal motivations have many layers.

Looking in the mirror and examining our reflection can be uncomfortable, eye-opening, and a little scary if we're honest with ourselves. Facing our own shortcomings, egos, and failures may be painful and produce feelings of shame or regret. However, we'll never be the authentic leader God created us to be if we don't shine that blinding light of truth into our own hearts. Only then can we identify the motivations we need God's help to change.

The first step to change is awareness, then confession, then accepting forgiveness. Then, and only then, does natural growth occur. And though the first pinprick of self-realization may very well produce shame, rest assured: God will not leave you there.

While it's much easier to just apply some leadership principles you find in a fortune cookie and fall back into a management mindset, Christ has called you to be more than a manager. He's called you to model Him and lead. But with that calling comes responsibility. To live a life bigger than yourself as a servant leader, you're responsible for being the person you want others to be. Moreover, your thoughts, feelings, and actions must be free of pride and ego-driven motivations.

While the Bible doesn't use the terms *manager, supervisor,* or *CEO,* I believe we can adapt the Bible's terminology to the marketplace we work in today. The early churches were made up of elders, teachers, and apostles with duties to lead, manage, and inspire others.

As the Church has expanded, we know that God calls us to use our place in this world as our ministry. The duties in your job description make no difference to God. Your title means very little. The industry doesn't matter either. *For such a time as this,* God placed you right where you are today. He's designed your relationships, your experiences, and your gifts to serve where you are. His plan is to work through you to develop those people that He has placed in your care. This is for the ultimate purpose of *"letting your light shine before men, so they will see your good work and glorify your Father in Heaven."*

If you're currently in a place of leadership, or you aspire to be, beware! James 3:1 warns us that those in leadership will be judged more harshly. While the only means of salvation (*by grace through faith in Jesus Christ,* as Paul tells us in Ephesians 2:8) applies to leaders and non-leaders alike, this doesn't mean God will judge you harshly—because we know that God is impartial. God isn't looking to smite people who don't live up to His expectations.

However, the **world** will judge leaders more harshly. Those who look to you for leadership will judge you. Those who listen to your words and watch your actions will judge you harshly. You'll never be perfect, but being an authentic version of yourself in the leadership role God has given you will allow your team to see you as a real person following a real God, striving to do what is right.

In my life—while working in ministry and in the secular world—I've met more leaders than I can count who didn't have their own lives in order. In fact, many of them had personal lives that were a devastated mess. To compensate, they made work the center of their lives as a way of protecting their egos. They were controlling, micromanaging, argumentative, and lacking all self-awareness.

These are the people who will work every weekend, send emails at 2:00 AM, come to work before the sun is up, and make everyone else feel inferior. Their personal life seems purposeless, and they don't understand their true identity. So they seek validation through career success.

This is a pretty good picture of a workaholic. Unfortunately, workaholics are often applauded in the workplace because their supervisors value their production above anything else. But your job should never—and could never—be your identity. Your identity is far greater than your paycheck or your rung on the career ladder.

If this person describes a member of your team, it must be addressed. This personality may show great productivity, but at what price? A person whose entire identity is work can become passive-aggressive and egocentric while refusing to be a part of the team. Their ego—or lack thereof—tells them they must be set apart from the rest for the spotlight to shine only on them.

This person can also suffer from a martyr complex, believing they're forced to sacrifice more than any other team member. Needless to say, this is not only unhealthy for the workaholic, but also for the team. Unfortunately, the person stuck in the workaholic mindset usually has no idea how badly their behavior affects the team.

Now, if the workaholic I just described is *you*—don't be ashamed. You're in the right place! Over the next several days, we'll gently peel back the layers of the onion that protect the all-mighty ego. We're going to invite God into those secret areas where only He can bring wholeness, healing, and growth.

You'll learn how to *"present yourself to God as one approved, a worker who has no need to be ashamed, rightly handling the word of truth,"* as 2 Timothy 2:15 instructs us.

But to be a worker who has no need to be ashamed, we'll need to dig in a little deeper. The book of *Titus* gives us a great starting point for self-examination. By modeling our leadership according to the standard described in Titus 1:6–9, we can become leaders who live without regret, guilt, or shame.

These verses tell us that a leader must be blameless and have one spouse. The leader's children must be faithful and not insubordinate. A leader must be God's steward: not self-willed, not quick-tempered, not violent, or given to wine. He should not be greedy. A leader should be hospitable, a lover of good, sober, just, holy, and self-controlled. A leader must have sound doctrine and be able to exhort others while convicting those who contradict… *Whew!*

Let's pause. There's a lot to unpack here!

Over the next ten days, we'll use this passage as our roadmap to becoming a leader according to God's standards. So, come prepared each day with a pen and a cup of coffee (or tea, if you prefer), and use these pages as a workbook.

The daily readings are purposefully designed to be short and sweet to allow God space to move in your unique heart and in your unique position in life. I recommend only processing one attribute of servant leadership each day.

Before reading, pray that the Holy Spirit would reveal truth to you and make you receptive to it. Then, as you go about your day, be mindful of your actions as they pertain to the leadership attribute, and meditate on your underlying motivations.

Let each day's reading be a time you enjoy with your loving Father. He wants to use *you* to change the world!

Reflection: Lord, I want to present myself to you as a worker who need not be ashamed. I want to serve you in all truth. I am opening my heart and my mind for you to change me……(finish this prayer in your own words)

Artwork Explained

"Writing in Dust" Leszek Forczek

Think about that moment. The townspeople and religious leaders had found a woman caught committing a terrible crime. They dragged her to Jesus to pass judgment. As the crowd stood with their bricks and stones raised over their heads, ready to crush this woman's body, Jesus paused. He simply paused and began drawing in the dust. He paused. When he finally spoke, his words were unexpected and cutting: "Whoever has no sin, cast the first stone." The angry crowd was forced to stop and take a moment of reflection. In that moment, they must have sensed the hypocrisy and knew they were no better than anyone else. It was a pivotal moment. I believe that's a moment every leader must face.

The first part of the book is all about self-discovery and searching our own hearts, because, as Paul said, "leaders should be blameless."

DAY 1

A Leader Must Be Blameless.

Well, that sounds impossible! After all, you're human, right? As humans, we're all bound to fail at times. The Lord knows that, and being blameless is not synonymous with being perfect. However, the Lord is calling us to lead by example.

James 3:1 warns us that those in leadership will be judged more harshly. This isn't to say God will smite leaders who don't live up to His expectations. And we know from *Ephesians 2:8* that our means of salvation (by grace through faith) applies to everyone equally—leaders and non-leaders alike. But the world does judge leaders more harshly. Leaders tend to live in the spotlight, and those who listen to you and watch you will certainly be critical if your words and actions don't align.

The Lord calls us to lead by example, and the opposite of leading by example is hypocrisy. Hypocrisy is claiming to believe something your actions contradict or don't support. It comes from the Greek word that actually means "actor" or "to wear a mask." We remember what Jesus said to leaders of His time who were hypocritical. In *Luke 11:46* He said, "You load men with heavy burdens but you yourself do not touch the burden. Woe to you! You blind guides!"

Let's translate this into modern-day workplace English: "You sit in your corner office making burdensome rules and telling everyone else what to do. Yet you yourself will not get off your backside and help! You're going to regret that!"

In contrast, Paul gives us great advice in *1 Thessalonians 3:11*: "Live a quiet life. Mind your own business. Work with your own hands and you will lack nothing."

Hypocrisy will destroy any healthy culture. Remember, a while back we talked about people in leadership being judged more harshly. This is a perfect example of that judgment in the team you lead. If you don't abide by the same rules you put in place for your team, or if you don't enforce the rules with impartiality, your team will judge you.

Not only that, your team won't trust you. Building trust is based on honesty, and if your actions and your words are not in alignment, you'll soon find your team won't follow your lead. They'll start telling you what you want to hear while they do the opposite or hide the evidence of their actions. The boundaries become blurred, and your team won't feel safe. As a servant leader, you must consistently model the expectations.

Think of examples of hypocrisy we see in our world today and the way it has eroded our trust. We've seen politicians denounce corruption while accepting bribes. People who profess to be tolerant yet alienate those who disagree with them. Religious leaders who preach purity yet cheat on their spouse. Think how these people have tarnished not only their own reputations, but have also shaded our collective view of government, organized religion, and public leaders in general.

Your mission deserves better. Trust and reputation will be the cornerstone of your leadership if you do what you say, say what you mean, and mean what you say.

So while you'll never be perfect, you can lead by example and be authentically *you* in the leadership role God has given you. Then your team will see you as a real person, following a real God, striving to do what's right. The opposite of leading by example is hypocrisy—and hypocrisy will destroy a healthy workplace culture.

We live in a world that's noisy and full of distractions. We must choose to make the leadership of our people a clear priority. You have heard the phrase, "mind your own business". Leading your team is your business. It's easy to get distracted and to spend more time minding someone else's business rather than our own. Then possibly we may pass our own work off for someone else to do, and we will lose strength in our position. Instead, concern your mind with what you need to be concerned with doing, **growing as a leader**, and you will find your focus becoming crystal clear.

Reflect

What are some company policies you don't agree with?

_____

_____

_____

_____

_____

_____

Do you enforce them anyway?

_____

_____

_____

_____

_____

_____

Do you follow the rules you enforce for others?

_____

_____

_____

_____

_____

_____

_____

Do you gossip or talk about people on your team?

_____

_____

_____

_____

_____

_____

_____

Are you honest? Do you own up to your mistakes or hide behind a mask of perfection?

_____

_____

_____

_____

_____

_____

_____

When you reflect on *1 Thessalonians 3:11*, what would this look like in your own life? Is your life too noisy?

_____

_____

_____

_____

_____

_____

_____

_____

_____

Do you waste time getting involved in business that doesn't concern you?

_____

_____

_____

_____

_____

_____

_____

Are you micromanaging your team, or do they know you trust them?

_____

_____

_____

_____

_____

_____

_____

Close in Prayer:

Lord, lead me today in seeing myself in all truth. Please quiet my busy mind to hear your voice. Test my motivations and make me pure....

_____

_____

_____

_____

_____

_____

_____

_____

_____

_____

_____

_____

_____

_____

_____

_____

_____

_____

_____

_____

_____

_____

_____

_____

DAY 2

A Leader Must Have One Spouse And Faithful Children.

"If anyone does not provide for his relatives, and especially for members of his household, he has denied the faith and is worse than an unbeliever."

1 Timothy 5:8 (ESV)

The provision referenced in this verse is not just about money and paying the bills. Providing for your family requires love, energy, discipline, and a plethora of other duties that require you to be present. Working overtime and coming home useless every day is not providing for the needs of your family. You can't use your position at work as an excuse to deny your first responsibility, which is to your family.

Being married more than once doesn't discredit you from being a good leader. Your past failures or successes are just that—in the past. They bear no weight on your future unless you haven't learned the lessons that were provided for you. You can only focus on the life that you have today. As you take the beautiful lessons from the past, even the painful ones, and apply them to your future, you prove that you have gained wisdom.

You may have children that are less than obedient. Is Paul suggesting that those with unfaithful children can't be trusted to lead others outside of their family if they can't lead and have control over their own? Maybe.

Every parent experiences regret when they look back on the times that they didn't provide everything they should have for their children. Those moments will break your heart. It's never too late. It's never too late to make those relationships a priority and to establish the boundaries that God wants you to place around your family. Your ability to lead is going to be greatly affected and distracted when your home is unsettled. Your hand is going to be forced to choose your leadership at work or your leadership at home. One is going to suffer.

Every person, in leadership or not, has family dynamics and issues that will arise. As a leader, you will earnestly desire to give 100% to your work, but then as a loving spouse, parent, or adult child, you want to give 100% to your family. You don't have 200% to give. You are one person.

The fulcrum theory of time management is borrowed from physics. The fulcrum is the pivot point of the lever. Imagine a seesaw. At times, the fulcrum is perfectly in the middle and both sides are equal. Work is good. Family is good. You are right in the middle, as the fulcrum, holding up both sides equally.

Then, there is a crisis at work. You are losing money or staff. The new project has just blown up. Your boss is coming in for inspections. The fulcrum has to move to balance the weight on one side of the seesaw. Your focus and energy must concentrate on work fully to bring back the balance—but just for a little while, and then you can come back to center.

Until the next situation. You get the call that your spouse is sick or your child is suspended from school. The fulcrum has to be repositioned. This is the dance of balance. If your family is continually in a state of flux, out of control, or disintegrating, you have no business trying to be a leader outside of your home. Your first obligation is caring for the blessing of those people.

As a single mom raising a son, I had to make that conscious choice every single day to put steel boundaries around my time with my son. It would've been very easy to justify working around the clock to pay the bills. While I did work three jobs for most of those years, I chose positions that allowed me flexibility to put my little family first. It meant denying promotions and cutting coupons, but it was only for a season. You will never regret the time you dedicate to your family.

You've been trusted with many things. God has given you incredible resources and blessings. You have 24 hours every day. You have a mind and a Spirit that is strong. You have a heart that He tells you to guard. You have countless material blessings surrounding you. And most importantly, you have the people in your world. Those people may be your family of origin, the family that you married and procreated, or it may be the family of friends placed in your sphere. Guard what has been given to you and show God that you can be trusted with these blessings.

Reflect

Are you running to work so that you can avoid a difficult situation at home?

_____

_____

_____

_____

_____

_____

_____

Have you missed important family events because you thought your job was more important?

_____

_____

_____

_____

_____

_____

_____

Do you feel guilty for time you have lost with your loved ones for work?

_____

_____

_____

_____

_____

_____

_____

Do you feel important to your family for more than a paycheck?

_____

_____

_____

_____

_____

_____

_____

Where is your fulcrum currently? What do you need to do to get back to center?

_____

_____

_____

_____

_____

_____

_____

_____

DAY 3

A Leader Must Be A Good Steward.

The *Holman Bible Dictionary* defines a steward as "someone who utilizes and manages all of the resources God has provided for His glory and for the betterment of creation." We are collaborators with God in our work. Therefore, we have to thoughtfully choose to maintain and wisely use the resources God has given us. Those resources encompass a lot—everything, in fact. Our time, talents, associates, our home, office supplies, vehicle, family… and the list goes on.

If you're wealthy, don't be proud or trust in the money. Instead, we should trust in the one who gives. God wants us to enjoy life and all that He gives us. But that also comes with the responsibility of sharing those things. We need to hold our blessings with an open hand and diligently look for ways to share and to give. At any moment, we should be ready to open our purse strings to those in need.

Sharing the money we have is one of the simplest ways we can be generous with others and with God. But it doesn't end there. God doesn't need your money, and neither does your team. What God really wants—and what your team needs—is your heart. You give your heart to God when you trust His word and act in loving obedience.

You show love to your team by using your gifts to support them. Love is an action verb. Your heart will be visible in the things you do, the words you speak, and the attention you give to those around you. Being a servant leader means serving others with everything you have at your disposal. In doing so, you're being a good steward of everything God has given to you by using your gifts to bless others, rather than hoarding them.

I believe our greatest and most valuable resource is something we all have. We all have an equal amount of this resource in a day. It's our time. Because I value this resource so much, it's the one I've struggled the most to give. I admit, I like lazy days. I like being selfish with my time and sometimes want to simply do nothing. I'm guilty of wasting countless hours scrolling my phone, watching fruitless entertainment, and playing inane games on my phone. To justify this,

I tell myself the lie, "I deserve this time since I work so hard." I'll never get those hours back, and my only prayer can be that God would redeem my time.

Yes, our human body and mind need rest to function optimally. We need time to get our batteries charged and our energies refreshed. But neither you nor I "deserve" this leisure time any more than we deserve to spend someone else's money. And while "me time" is not inherently bad, it's not something we should feel entitled to. Just like an abundance of money is a blessing to hold with an open hand, so is an abundance of leisure time. Our days on this earth and the hours in them belong to the one who made them.

So, I challenge you to open your schedule to the unscheduled. Those unscheduled encounters with God and with people are often filled with purpose and wonderful surprises. We limit what we can do—and what God can do through us—when we set imaginary boundaries around our "selfish" time. When I put more value into my time than I do God's time, there's no way I'll complete the good works God has prepared for me to do.

"Each of you should use whatever gift you have received to serve others, as faithful stewards of God's grace."

1 Peter 4:10

Close in Prayer:

Lord, I confess that everything I own, or think I own, belongs to you. You have entrusted me with much. Help me to be faithful with every single thing I have at my disposal so that you may find me trustworthy.

Reflect

What resources do you have outside of money?

_____

_____

_____

_____

_____

_____

_____

Honestly consider, have you ever skimmed from company funds? Maybe taking home office supplies, wasting work time on personal business, or using your position for gain in your personal life?

_____

_____

_____

_____

_____

_____

_____

Do you live in a generous manner or is there some place you would like to give more?

_____

_____

_____

_____

_____

_____

_____

Do you think you're using the resource of your time wisely? How would you like to manage it better?

_____
_____
_____
_____
_____
_____
_____

What resources are you depleting?

_____
_____
_____
_____
_____
_____

In what areas of your life do you need to re-evaluate your stewardship?

_____
_____
_____
_____
_____
_____
_____
_____
_____

Close in Prayer:

I encourage you to finish this prayer in your own words, but first ask God to reveal truth to you about yourself.

Lord, you have created good works for me to do. Please open my eyes to see these works as it pertains to the people in my life. Forgive me for taking these people for granted. Please open those lines of communication for us and make my mind fully present.

_____

_____

_____

_____

_____

_____

_____

_____

_____

_____

_____

_____

_____

_____

_____

_____

_____

_____

_____

DAY 4

A Leader Must Not Be Self-Willed

A self-willed person is someone who is headstrong, stubborn, independent, and not willing to yield to other opinions or wishes. Some Bible translations replace the word "self-willed" with "overbearing."

As a leader, there will be times when you'll have to dig in your heels and hold your ground to move the mission forward. But these moments should be approached with humility, rather than with "self-willed" traits like pride or arrogance. In this way, you'll be acting in a "mission-willed" manner, ensuring the team succeeds at accomplishing its mission.

At the same time, being peaceable, gentle, and willing to yield is paramount, when it's appropriate. Wise leaders know when to yield their own will to benefit the organization's mission and its people. If you allow your pride to lead, you'll find your organization rooted in disputes, fighting, and mistrust.

As King Solomon warns in Proverbs 26:12, *"Do you see a man wise in his own eyes? There is more hope for a fool than for him."* Acknowledge when you don't have all the answers, and be willing to ask lots of questions. You'll learn more about your company by talking to your front-line staff than having lunch with the CEO any day. It's with your front-line staff that you'll find most of the answers for creating systems, identifying roadblocks to achieving goals, and exposing the underbelly of customer dissatisfaction.

You have to be humble enough to know that your way of doing things is not the only way, and may not be the best way. Your team, with all of their ideas and experiences, are your greatest source of wisdom. If you're willing to be open-minded to the input of others, your company will grow!

Close in Prayer:

Lord, not my will but your will be done. Help me to put my own ambitions and ideas in perspective. Be Lord of my life and Lord of my will. Forgive me for my rebellion and self-serving motives...

Reflect

Has your pride led you into an argument?

_____

_____

_____

_____

_____

_____

_____

Do you put the needs of the team ahead of your own?

_____

_____

_____

_____

_____

_____

_____

Are you more concerned with furthering your career or advancing the mission of the company?

_____

_____

_____

_____

_____

_____

_____

Are you more concerned with furthering your own career or the careers of the people you serve?

_____

_____

_____

_____

_____

_____

_____

Who will you talk to today to find different ways of doing the job? Someone with a different perspective then yours. Why that person?

_____

_____

_____

_____

_____

_____

_____

_____

Close in Prayer:

I encourage you to finish this prayer in your own words, but first ask God to reveal truth to you about yourself.

Lord, you have created good works for me to do. Please open my eyes to see these works as it pertains to the people in my life. Forgive me for taking these people for granted. Please open those lines of communication for us and make my mind fully present.

_____

_____

_____

_____

_____

_____

_____

_____

_____

_____

_____

_____

_____

_____

_____

_____

_____

_____

_____

_____

DAY 5

A Leader Must Not Be Quick-Tempered.

"A fool gives full vent to his anger, but a wise man keeps himself under control."

Proverbs 29:11 (NIV)

Employees need a sense of stability that comes from predictability within the organization and its leadership. But a quick-tempered person is unpredictable and displays a lack of self-control. No one willingly follows such a leader.

Leaders who allow emotions like anger or frustration to overtake logic and composure will never successfully win the confidence and trust of their people. Their quick temper not only creates a sense of instability, but also causes emotional discomfort in others. Unbridled emotions lead to an unbridled tongue, and the damaging effects of words spoken in anger will ripple through an organization, creating a culture of mistrust, fear, and conflict-avoidance. Tiptoeing around your supervisor is no way to work or live.

As leaders, we have to encourage healthy conflict in order to grow. A healthy culture means that all associates feel safe to share their ideas, even if they conflict with management. Those beautiful and unique opinions will take your organization to new heights. A foundation of trust starts with being quick to listen and slow to speak.

A gentle word will defuse anger.

Proverbs 15:1

In every tough conversation, you want to avoid an argument at all costs. Because if you lose, you lose. And oftentimes, even if you win, you lose. Jesus told us that we need to *"agree with our adversary quickly"* before the situation escalates.

Always begin difficult conversations in an open and friendly way. Welcome civil disagreement, then listen. Just listen, and avoid those impulses to butt in or get defensive. Ask lots of questions. After you've heard everything they have to say, thank the person for showing you a different perspective. Look for the places where you agree.

One of the greatest de-escalating sentences I use is, "I don't blame you for feeling the way you do. If I were in your situation, I might feel the same way." Be honest about any mistakes you've made, as this will make the other person less defensive. Try to keep the focus on the facts, and if you're wrong, admit it. Doing this requires locking our natural emotions in a box, secured with a chain, and tossed into a vault.

Reflect

Do you often speak without thinking because of emotion?

_____

_____

_____

_____

_____

_____

_____

Do you need to apologize to someone for words or actions you regret?

_____

_____

_____

_____

_____

_____

Can you have a difficult conversation about someone's conduct without yelling, insulting, or getting angry?

_____

_____

_____

_____

_____

_____

_____

Close in Prayer:

Father, forgive me for all of the moments when I have allowed my pride, ego, and emotions to hurt other people and my relationships. Help me, Lord, to approach every situation with love today so that you can work through me. Please make me approachable and open-minded. Help me to be your hands and feet today.

_____

_____

_____

_____

_____

_____

_____

_____

_____

_____

_____

_____

_____

_____

_____

_____

_____

_____

_____

_____

_____

DAY 6

A Leader Must Not Be Given To Wine.

There are hundreds of sermons on the internet that will give you differing insights into the Biblical view of drinking alcohol. I'll let you research that for yourself, as I don't pretend to be a Biblical scholar. Frankly, that is between you and your Creator. But I believe most would agree that drinking and thinking don't go well together.

When you watch movies or TV shows from the 70's and 80's, you'll notice every executive had a bar in their office, and they would chat about their two-martini lunches. I'm not sure how any work actually got done after noon if lunch consisted of vodka and olives. But lack of productivity is the least of the detrimental effects alcohol can have on our careers and workplace relationships.

We've all heard tales of those Christmas office parties gone horribly wrong. Co-workers drinking together will usually lead to words being spoken that are best left for our private relationships. Respect can be lost, and that embarrassment can destroy a career. But furthermore, as we discussed yesterday, employees will rightly find it hard to trust a leader who isn't in control of themselves—whether the leader becomes consumed by emotion or by the effects of alcohol.

Paul's choice of words on this subject in Titus is interesting to me. To be "given to wine" implies the person has given up their self-control. They have given themselves over to a substance, which is now controlling them.

Our current HR directors would not approve of an office bar or cocktails at lunch, so drinking at work likely isn't an issue for most people. But what's your relationship with alcohol after work, or on the weekends? Are you in control, or do you hand alcohol the reins?

I personally enjoy good wine or a fun happy hour with friends more than most, and I wrestle with lining up my behaviors with what I believe God wants. God's commands for our behavior are based in his infinite wisdom as our Creator; he knows what's best for the humans he designed. He's given us the Old and New Testaments, which are chock-full of sound advice for a good life, whether you're a Christian or not. So we know there's nothing good about excessive alcohol. There's no positive physiological outcome.

Being "given" to alcohol will deteriorate our health. It'll deteriorate our brains. Being hungover makes us lazy and unproductive. Drunkenness can lead to debauchery, which leads to embarrassment and loss of respect. Loss of self-control can jeopardize the things we hold dear, like relationships or possessions. The book of Proverbs tells us that being drunk will lead to seeing strange things, and our brains will think things that aren't true. We'll babble. We'll have wounds that we don't know where they came from, and we will have red eyes. Yep, been there, own that T-shirt. Maybe you can relate as well.

If you're feeling conviction, shame, or guilt about your drinking habits, God can help you take back control over alcohol. He has power over everything. And once you've asked God to help you regain control, I'd suggest getting honest about your situation and your habits with someone you trust. We're only as sick as our secrets. Once you speak the words you're afraid to say, healing can begin.

Reflect

Is there a substance that has affected your job performance negatively?

_____

_____

_____

_____

_____

_____

_____

Can you think of a person whose life was destroyed by alcohol or drugs? How did it start and how did it end?

_____

_____

_____

_____

_____

_____

_____

Are there any moments in your life when you know an addiction led to regret?

_____

_____

_____

_____

_____

_____

_____

Close in Prayer:

Lord, you know everything. You know my secrets. I agree with you that a substance has affected my life. You have given me the power of a sound mind and I am the righteousness of Christ through the power of the Holy Spirit. I need your Holy Spirit now! Strengthen my will and remove any desire to drink and do anything to dull my senses. Help me to serve you fully today and every day of my life.

_____
_____
_____
_____
_____
_____
_____
_____
_____
_____
_____
_____
_____
_____
_____
_____
_____
_____
_____
_____

DAY 7

A Leader Should Not Be Violent.

Isn't it interesting that Paul calls out a quick temper and violence in this verse as separate characteristics? Being quick-tempered can lead to violence, but it's not the same. Violence includes a physical force—a force that's intended to damage or hurt someone or something. Violence intimidates and scares people, and that's the intent. It can be fist-banging on the desk, or a chair flying across the room. It can be a puffed-up chest and red face that makes someone cower.

Paul tells us to avoid this, for obvious reasons that would include jail time, lawsuits, and injury to ourselves and others that we might regret. But for leaders this is especially important. Leaders should not abuse their position of authority and power by inflicting violence upon others, whether physical or emotional.

Violence is a physical behavior intended to hurt. While punching an annoying co-worker may be tempting, most of us would not act on that temptation. But slamming a door, screaming, or cussing can be seen as violence. The behavior of leaders is typically on display for many to see, and it should model desirable traits for others in the organization. And again, Paul's words implore leaders to be self-controlled in order to command the respect and trust of subordinates and peers. It's a strong caution not to let emotions overwhelm you or a situation, or you risk losing respect and trust.

I've never been in a fight. Personally, I could never imagine myself physically striking another person. It's not in my DNA, maybe because I came from a family that didn't use corporal punishment. That doesn't mean I'm not prone to physically lashing out. Every time a car cuts me off in traffic and drives below the speed limit when I am late for work, it takes every ounce of strength to keep my hands at 10 and 2 and my middle finger in the car.

Jesus said in Matthew 5:38-39, "You have heard that it was said, 'An eye for an eye and a tooth for a tooth.' But I say to you, Do not resist the one who is evil. But if anyone slaps you on the right cheek, turn to him the other also."

There are times when our human minds tell us violence is justified. We rightly want to fight evil and wrongdoing, and there's a time and place for that. These words of Jesus aren't meant to turn strong people into doormats, nor allow others to hurt us physically or emotionally. I believe Jesus is warning us about plotting revenge. Your mind and your emotions will be bitter. When bitterness takes hold of us, it will taint all of our relationships. Instead, we turn the other cheek and let God take care of vengeance. No matter how desperately I want that other driver on the road to know their wrongdoing, I have to trust that God is a better instructor than my middle finger.

Reflect

What are moments that make you so upset that your body reacts in an illogical way?

_____

_____

_____

_____

_____

_____

_____

Do you ever feel you do not have control of your actions or reactions?

_____

_____

_____

_____

_____

_____

What tools or methods can you use to stop yourself before you react?

_____

_____

_____

_____

_____

_____

_____

Close in Prayer:

Father, I need your Spirit to take control when I feel out of control. In those moments when anger swells inside of me, remind me of your love. Remind me that others are watching me and I am called to be a good shepherd of this flock. Give me the courage to ask forgiveness to anyone I have harmed. I pray that my behavior reflects your nature today.

DAY 8

A Leader Should Not Be Greedy.

Luke 12:15 records Jesus' words: "Watch out! Be on your guard against all kinds of greed; a man's life does not consist in the abundance of his possessions." (NIV)

Greed is defined by Webster's Dictionary as an "intense selfish desire for something, especially wealth, power or food." Our culture has been overwhelmed with greedy politicians who have greased their own pockets with taxpayers' money and have used their influence to jeopardize the security of, and endanger, our country. No leader would want to be compared to a politician who succumbed to the blinding monster of greed.

The "me-first" world creates a monster. That monster will start as a seemingly innocent desire and turn into an insatiable appetite for more and more. Greed will numb our conscience and deceive us. How many people do you know who started their careers just wanting success and to provide well for their families, but, before long, chasing the accumulation of "stuff" robbed them of time and family?

The story of King Midas reminds us that greed will destroy. He simply wanted to turn everything he touched into gold, which is where we get the euphemism of having the "Midas touch". Soon everyone and everything he loved had turned to objects of gold, leaving him alone and empty. The testimony of Judas' life is a biblical tale of greed which started with him skimming out of the money box. But then it was his greed that led him to sell Jesus for 30 pieces of silver. The guilt of that greed led to his suicide.

Money, possessions, positions and food are certainly not bad things. It's when we crave these things in excess and for selfish reasons that we'll lose sight of our real purpose. Having selfish motivations is the antithesis of servant leadership. A servant leader doesn't seek personal gain for its own sake. Instead, a servant leader seeks ways for the team to gain wealth, power, and greater influence for the benefit of the organization.

Your team will smell the difference. Personal gain can't be hidden forever with strategic conversations or manipulation. Sooner or later, true motives are uncovered and trust is destroyed.

Greed often goes hand in hand with covetousness. To "covet" something means to want what someone else has. We've all done it. I wish I had her job. I wish I had his house. I wish I had a figure like she has. I wish I had a family like that. Nothing spits in the face of God's generosity more than coveting someone else's things.

When we let that daydream of having "x" keep lingering in our mind, we're turning "x" into an idol. We'll worship it, waste time and energy trying to obtain it, and create such a high pedestal for it that we'll destroy ourselves in the pursuit of our "x."

To rip out the root of greed, which I believe we are all born with, we need to continually check our motivations:

Why haven't I been home for dinner with my family in weeks? Is it because I'm desperately trying to make money my family needs, or am I trying to buy a boat bigger than my neighbor's?

Why do I send Christmas cards? Is it to spread love and well-wishes, or am I really hoping to get a lot of cards in return so I can display them on my mantle and feel important? Yes, I admit it!

Did I give that donation because I believe in the cause, or did I want people to admire my generosity? Yep, I've done that too.

Did I compliment her because I genuinely wanted to encourage her, or am I just trying to make her like me? Yeah, done that too.

Wanting to make a better salary or to be promoted to a position with greater influence is not inherently wrong. Making more money means greater opportunity for generosity. More influence puts us in a stronger position to change the world. Just always ask yourself, "Why do I want this?" and "Who (or what) am I serving?"

Reflect

Do you compare what you have to what other people have? If so, how does that make you feel?

_____

_____

_____

_____

_____

_____

_____

What selfless act have you done in the past, OR can you do for one of your teammates?

_____

_____

_____

_____

_____

_____

_____

What is your "x"?

_____

_____

_____

_____

_____

_____

_____

What is your goal professionally for the next 12 months? Why? List any ways you've been inauthentic in your motives to achieve personal gain. Then, ask God to forgive you.

_____

_____

_____

_____

_____

_____

_____

_____

Close in Prayer:

"Search me, O God, and know my heart! Try me and know my thoughts!" Psalm 139:23 (ESV)

Father, I know that every good and perfect gift comes from you. Forgive me for my lack of gratitude. Please remind me of all I have to be thankful for. Lead me to contentment and remove any greed or selfish ambition in my heart. Replace it with what you want for me……

_____

_____

_____

_____

_____

_____

_____

_____

_____

_____

_____

_____

_____

_____

_____

_____

_____

_____

_____

_____

_____

_____

DAY 9

A Leader Should Be Hospitable.

If you have the gift of hospitality, this may come easily for you. As you hear these words, you picture yourself throwing a party or cooking for the neighborhood. You love pot-luck dinners and tear through *Martha Stewart Living* magazines. You can create a charcuterie board two miles long and have an apron for every holiday.

This is one form of hospitality—opening our homes. But *Romans 12:10-13* gives a much bigger picture of hospitality. *"Be kindly affectionate to one another with brotherly love, in honor giving preference to one another... distributing to the needs of the saints, given to hospitality." (NKJV)* This form of hospitality is about opening our hearts to others, not just our homes.

Hospitality is about caring for the needs of others and practicing love as an action verb, not a warm and fuzzy emotion. It doesn't have to be a lavish dinner party. It can be as easy as inviting a co-worker to have a cup of coffee or to join you for lunch in the break room. Maybe you see the perfect gift for someone and give it to them when it's not expected. Most importantly, hospitality is also taking care of someone's needs.

Doing this in the workplace is transformative. Many companies will bolster the slogan, "We're family!" But where is the proving ground? Is the rubber hitting the road or is that slogan just another flat tire?

Dave Ramsey, financial guru and President of Crown Financial, is known for having one of the best company cultures anyone could dream of. He attributes that to the fact that he takes care of his people. One example of this was when an associate was diagnosed with cancer. She was horribly ill and could no longer continue to work. Instead of accepting her resignation, he continued to employ her even though she couldn't work. In his words, "She worked for me for 15 years. I had to take care of her." She continued to collect a paycheck for two years while going through chemo and regaining her strength. Dave Ramsey was simply taking care of the people as if they were family.

Thankfully, the associate recovered and returned to work. Imagine the impact of his generosity! The sick employee benefited, but a powerful message ripped through his organization! His staff knew they were valued as people, not just a means of profit.

Not every company can afford to do as Dave did for his employee, but we can use every resource we have to take care of our work-family.

Several months ago, a nurse at the community I manage had to leave her home because of domestic violence. Although she had a good job and found a place to live, she literally had nothing else. She bought a condo in foreclosure for $10,000 that didn't even have a floor, let alone appliances, but at least she had a roof over her head and could sleep without fear.

As a management team, or as a "family," we mobilized a mission to get her needs met. We reached out to our vendors, church groups, friends, and other co-workers. Within two weeks, she had a home she could feel comfortable in. A contractor fixed her floor. Beds, furniture and housewares were donated, and appliances were found on Facebook Marketplace. We brought the company vehicle to her door and unloaded everything on her wish list. As tears fell down her cheeks, she said, "Why would you do this for me?" The answer was simple. Because we ARE family!

Reflect

Has anyone ever shown you true hospitality?

_____

_____

_____

_____

_____

_____

_____

What does it mean to you to view love as an action verb?

_____

_____

_____

_____

_____

_____

_____

Would you like your workplace to feel more like a "family"?

_____

_____

_____

_____

_____

_____

_____

_____

What are your barriers to making that happen? Are there key players that you could meet with to form a strategy to create a family culture?

_____

_____

_____

_____

_____

_____

_____

_____

Close in Prayer:

Father, you have shown abundant hospitality to me. Remove the calluses from my heart and open my eyes to the people around me in need. Give me the will and the means to meet those needs, whether physical or emotional. I pray that you will change the culture where I work so that we will truly operate as a family should and help me to lead by example....

_____

_____

_____

_____

_____

_____

_____

_____

_____

_____

_____

_____

_____

_____

_____

_____

_____

_____

_____

_____

_____

_____

DAY 10

A Leader Should Love What Is Good.

In order for us to "love what is good," we first must define what God sees as "good." We must be able to discern the things that are truly good from those that merely appear to be good. We can get to know God and His definition of "good" by studying scripture. Then, we must pursue these good things. A person's heart is revealed by what he loves and, as we've discussed, love is an action verb. We show love by the amount of attention, time, and energy we devote to someone or something. Allow your values to be evident in what you choose, encourage and protect.

In *Romans 12:9-16*, we read that sincere love and devotion to one another are good things. In *Micah 6:8*, God says it's good to be kind, to love mercy and justice, and to walk humbly. But the enemy of truth will lie and try to trick us into believing something is "good." So we have to remain rooted in scripture and ask God for discernment.

A perfect example of human deception is Eve's experience with the snake in the garden. Satan gave her a perfectly rational argument for why she should eat the forbidden fruit. He told her all of the "good" things that would come from her choice. She would have superior knowledge. She would think like God. How could that be bad?

Haven't we all rationalizeda behavior that is contrary to God's will? "Well, if I cheat on my taxes, I can save a lot of money and give it to the church!" "I'm not going to church today because it'll give me more time to spend with my family." "I know the new associate needs more training, but I'm so busy. She will learn on her feet." "If I hold people to a higher standard, it could cause contention, so it's best to just avoid confrontation." The list can go on forever.

Ultimately, the money never goes to the church and the time for family is wasted in chores. The associate gets frustrated from lack of understanding and quits. So now you're ridiculously busy. And from lack of accountability, your team has no guardrails. You become disconnected from the people, and you live in disharmony with others bringing you down.

If you give up what you want most for what you want now, you're being deceived. You want a deeper relationship with God, but you also want to stay in bed. You want a better relationship with your children, but you also don't feel like making dinner. You want to be successful at work, but you also want to take a blue sky holiday. You want a thriving culture, but you don't really want to deal with confrontation.

Discerning good takes emotional intelligence and honesty. We can all agree that church, family, charity are good things. But in that day-to-day gray area where we have to make quick decisions and lead with authority, confidently acting on what's good is pivotal to the team's success and to your leadership. What do we do when the noise of the world and the limitations of our mind blind us from discernment?

God said. Period. God said do not eat, or even touch, that fruit. We may not fully understand why God tells us to do or not do something. We just have to know He said it. Read His words and believe them. When we don't know if something is truly good or not, go back to His words. God said. Praying for wisdom every single day is the most powerful act we do as a leader. In the book of James, we read that if anyone lacks wisdom, we can just ask God for it, and He promises to deliver!

Lastly, celebrating good things builds a cohesive team while setting a clear example of behaviors to model. As a leader, you'll find it wonderfully liberating to walk around your business looking for associates doing good. Focus the majority of your communication on the good.

During our monthly all-staff meetings, I developed a simple formula. In a typical meeting, the first 10 minutes are meant to inspire the staff to connect personally to the mission of the company and to live for something bigger than themselves. The next 20 minutes is all about celebrating! We celebrate sales, income, new associates, goals reached, and positive customer experiences in detail, focusing on the associates who were involved in these wins. The next 15 minutes focus on education, policy compliance, and overall housekeeping announcements. We end by celebrating associates' anniversaries and birthdays. Then we eat cake! During cake time, authentic conversations and celebrating wins and milestones unify the team and encourage them to strive for even greater success.

Reflect

If God were telling you about the good things in your life, what would He say?

_____

_____

_____

_____

_____

_____

_____

Have you justified a behavior that you knew was not what God wanted you to do?

_____

_____

_____

_____

_____

_____

_____

_____

What can you do today to create a culture of celebrating the good?

_____

_____

_____

_____

_____

_____

_____

_____

Close in Prayer:

Father, you alone are good. Give me wisdom to know what is right and good. Empower me to choose good. Through your Holy Spirit, give me eyes to see a bigger picture of what you want most in my life. Help me to model and celebrate all that is good in my family and in my position. Humbly use me to bring out the good in everyone I meet today....

DAY 11

A Leader Should Be Self-Disciplined.

The psychology of self-discipline involves controlling our impulses, emotions and thoughts. We need to be able to regulate these to achieve our goals as individuals and leaders. Every short-term goal leads to reaching the long-term goals. We can only envision those goals when we look at the bigger picture. Self-discipline and success go hand in hand.

If you're not self-controlled, then who or what is controlling you? That question hurts a little. How many times have I told myself that I won't snack on chips and cheese puffs? Yet, come 2:00 PM, I'm at the vending machine—sometimes buying more than one bag. It's a habit. A habit that I love in the moment. But after the second or third bag of chips, I feel gross, both physically and mentally.

So, why did I do it? Why do we stay up too late or drink too much? Why do we neglect exercise and hydration? Why do we keep circling that same destructive habit like a moth to a flame? Easy answer. It's inertia.

The law of inertia says an object in motion will stay in motion until it's countered with an outside force. Inertia is comfortable. It's a pattern where we've found a groove. We circle that groove over and over. And no matter how much we may want to jump off the tilt-a-whirl, no matter how much we know this behavior pattern isn't what we want, we'll continue to be pushed by invisible inertia until that motion is met with an outside force.

Inertia is the exact opposite of self-control or self-discipline. We operate in inertia when we're reluctant to change or are even afraid of change. Fortunately, the force of self-discipline will stop you from operating in a state of mindlessness. God created your brain to have enormous neuroplasticity—the ability to change and create new patterns.

Think of neuroplasticity in these terms: imagine a thick forest, and every day you have walked one path through the trees. That path would be pretty worn down, easy to locate, and simple to walk through each day. Now, imagine you want to take a different path. That first day would be a little challenging as you trudge through tall grasses and hack away at tree limbs to forge a new path. But the next day, it would be a little easier. By the time you walk that new path 10 or 20 times, it would be pretty easy—and at the same time, the first path will have become overgrown with weeds. You wouldn't find it again as easily.

Paul acknowledges our brain's ability to create new, better pathways in *Romans 12:2*. He says *"Do not conform to the pattern of this world, but be transformed by the renewing of your mind."* If you've ever been in a mental rut, thank God for creating our minds with the ability to be transformed!

Discipline is fundamental for all consistent practices and is the gateway to maturity. It is the force that can push you down a new path you know to be better. And fortunately, your own mind can generate this force! But if you haven't asserted control or discipline upon yourself in a while, it may not be easy to do at first. And if you struggle, you're certainly not alone. But the good news is self-discipline is like a muscle—the more you use it, the stronger it becomes. The less you use it, the more it will atrophy.

So what can you do today to halt the mindless inertia and put yourself on the path to accomplishing your goals?

1. First, pray. Ask the Holy Spirit to strengthen your self-control, which is a fruit of the Spirit as we see in *Galatians 5:23*. Ask God to renew your mind each day (*Romans 12:2*), and to help you focus your attention on the things of God, not of the flesh (*Colossians 3:2*).

2. Now, start with short-term goals that will provide quicker validation and boost your confidence. For instance, commit to going to bed early just for tonight. In the morning, you'll immediately feel the difference. Another option may be taking a walk after dinner instead of eating dessert. Try it tonight and see how you feel. Once you master a couple of these small goals, use discipline for something bigger like controlling your impulse to gossip or to be sarcastic.

3. Find an accountability partner! This is another great external force that can counteract the inertia of your existing habits.

Soon, you'll start to realize there's nothing stopping you and you are in control!

Reflect

Do you feel guilty about a habit? Is there something you feel is out of your control?

_____

_____

_____

_____

_____

_____

_____

In what areas of your life are you operating by inertia?

_____

_____

_____

_____

_____

_____

_____

Where do you need more power and strength in your life?

_____

_____

_____

_____

_____

_____

_____

Is there something that's controlling you?

_____

_____

_____

_____

_____

_____

_____

What choices do you want to change?

_____

_____

_____

_____

_____

_____

_____

What are two short-term goals you're going to accomplish today or this week, practicing self-discipline?

_____

_____

_____

_____

_____

_____

_____

_____

_____

Close in Prayer:

Lord, I need you. I need your strength to have power over my choices. Help me to live intentionally. Show me how to control myself and my behaviors. Lord, what do you want me to change today? (Give him time to speak and write down his answer)

_____

_____

_____

_____

_____

_____

_____

_____

_____

_____

_____

_____

_____

_____

_____

_____

_____

_____

_____

_____

_____

_____

DAY 12

A Leader Should Be Holy.

'Holy' is a very Christian word. It's a word that describes God, and the Bible actually says that **only** God is holy. So, how can we, as mere mortals, succeed at being holy?

Being holy literally means "to be set apart for honorable use." As Christians, we're set apart—hopefully by living a lifestyle that is different from the world's standards. We're not slaves to our desires. Instead, one day, one choice at a time, we turn from our old lives to be more like Jesus. It's a pursuit that we'll never master until we take our last breath on this planet.

Webster says that to be "holy" is to be "living with a highly moral or spiritual purpose." I love that definition! Because if you're in a place of leadership, anywhere in your world, you do have a morally high purpose! But just being in leadership doesn't make you holy, no more than being in a hospital makes you a doctor.

Being holy in your workplace or place of leadership means doing all of the other things we have discussed in this book, or at least striving to do all of them. Living in a way that's authentic, blameless, and loving toward others; being willing to set the standard for morals, work ethic, and excellence—that's being holy in your place of leadership. That's fulfilling your moral or spiritual purpose as a leader. As a leader, you have been set apart. Now, walk in a way that's worthy of the calling!

"Let your light so shine before men, that they will see your good works and glorify your God, who is in heaven." Matthew 5:16

Reflect

Do you feel holy?

_____

_____

_____

_____

_____

_____

_____

Do you think that God sees you as holy?

_____

_____

_____

_____

_____

_____

_____

How are you set apart and different from this world?

_____

_____

_____

_____

_____

_____

_____

_____

How can you tangibly be holy at your place of leadership?

_____

_____

_____

_____

_____

_____

_____

_____

Close in Prayer:

Lord, thank you that when you see me, you're looking through the lens of Jesus' blood. I want to live worthy of my calling and worthy of His sacrifice, but I need your help. You have set me apart for a purpose, but I struggle. Forgive me for the multitude of times that I have missed the target. By your grace, I will keep moving forward and striving to *honor* you. *How can I be set apart and holy today? (Give Him time to Speak)*

_____

_____

_____

_____

_____

_____

_____

_____

_____

_____

_____

_____

_____

_____

_____

_____

_____

END OF PART ONE

PART TWO

Artwork Explained

The Watercolor Painting "Return to the Sun" by Leszek Forczek

The monarch butterfly. It represents the concept of change: that the flapping of a butterfly's wings can change the wind on the other side of the world. We all start out as a caterpillar. Every caterpillar holds its strong and magnificent wings deep inside, but it must go through the process and hard work of the chrysalis before it can fly.

You've gone through the work of the cocoon these last weeks… now, it's time to stretch your wings!

Introduction to Part 2

You've spent the last two weeks allowing God to sharpen your self-awareness and shape your motivations as a servant leader. My prayer for you is that you've realized the unique and powerful position in which God has placed you. I also pray that God has used this time to make you more like him as you learn to serve others as a leader living by example.

Before we move on to the next 7 days of implementing servant leadership, let's reflect on the work that was done in your heart over the last two weeks.

What changes have you noticed in your own behavior or attitudes?

_____

_____

_____

_____

_____

_____

_____

The most impactful thing you can do as a servant leader is to be present. Be aware of everything and everyone in your field of vision. Be deliberate in your choice of words, facial expressions, and actions. And talk to your heavenly Father throughout your day. You may ask him 100 times a day, "How do you want me to serve this person?"

You're a servant leader when you work to push others into being the best version of themselves. You protect them. You see their needs. You see their areas for growth. You recognize their beautiful talents and experiences. You put the spotlight on them instead of nominating yourself to sing the solo. You wholeheartedly value and deeply know every member of the flock.

What do you need to work on to be a better servant leader?

_____

_____

_____

_____

_____

_____

_____

Once your heart's motivations to lead your team align with God's plan for your leadership, the culture of your organization will feel like family. It won't happen overnight, but be patient.

What changes have you seen in your organization since you started making servant leadership a priority? What changes have you noticed in your relationships?

Over the next 7 days, you'll be given practical steps to evaluate your leadership and begin embracing the great calling on your life. You'll also see how the Bible, and especially the apostle Paul, has so much to say about leadership and how you can apply the Bible to your job.

And when you complete this next week, don't stop learning! Pick up your Bible each day and as you read, ask God, "How does this apply to leadership?"

Is there a Bible verse that inspires you as a servant leader? If you don't have one, make it a priority to find one. Write it down and hang it in your car, put it on your desk, post it on your bathroom mirror, and tattoo it on your heart.

My Verse:

DAY 1

Manage Your Mindset

"Praise the Lord, o my soul, and forget not all his benefits."

Psalm 103:2 (KJV)

God is so understanding of our feeble minds. He knows we need to be reminded of his goodness. He gently invites us to worship him, knowing that in those pure moments of worship we remember. We become aware of the mighty presence of God, the presence that is always with us, though we forget.

We forget the excitement we experienced when we first came to know him. We forget the fire in our belly that drove us to devour his word when we first accepted him and were aware of his love for us. We forget all of the moments when God rescued us from devastation.

Isn't this true for so many things in our life? When you first met your spouse, you may have been intrigued by them. Opposites attract in dating, yet they seem to attack when married. It used to be exciting to have a romantic date night with your spouse, but maybe now it seems like a chore. Why spend the money when we can just rent a movie and get takeout?

When I first moved to Florida, I was overwhelmed by the beauty of the beach and how accessible it was. I could walk on the beach day or night, anytime, and I would be instantly aware of how small I am and how big our God is. I would spend an entire day just soaking up the warmth of the sun and the peace of the waves, praying and reading the Bible. It was magical to me.

Several years later, my friend in NY casually asked me, "When was the last time you were at the beach?" I had to take a long pause to rewind my memory that far back. After scanning the last months, and more months, I answered her, "It's been over two years." I lived 10 minutes from the ocean, yet hadn't been there in two years! Not only did I take for granted the fact that the ocean would always be there, but it had become mundane. More than mundane—it became inconvenient. Going to the beach meant packing the cooler, carrying a chair and beach bag, getting sand in the car. It just seemed like a chore. *"Forget not my benefits..."*

Does any of this sound familiar?

How about your job? You may have dreamed about being where you are today. You thought it would be the pinnacle. Do you remember how excited you were on your first day? Do you remember all the hopes you had and the plans you drafted? The day you found out you got that promotion, or the raise that made you feel like you had struck the lottery?

How do you feel now? Are you excited to go to work? Does that corner office that was once the thing of your dreams feel like a fishbowl now? Or worse yet, maybe it feels like a casket—small and claustrophobic. The luster has rubbed off of that pearl as your to-do list fills with tasks that no longer fulfill but only drain you.

This is a natural human experience, but it can—and must—be overcome!

Because longevity is important. Without longevity, you can't have a sustained positive impact as a leader in your organization. You'll need resilience—or what I call stick-to-itiveness—in tough situations or boring ones! I love the word *stick-to-itiveness*. I don't know who coined that word, but it paints a great picture. Stick to it!

Building a strong foundation and positive momentum takes time and patience. This means we may have to do some of the same small tasks over and over and over every day, and we may get bored. Every job has tasks we love to complete—ones that excite us—but also tasks that we just have to cross off the list. The problem is when we stop creating things that excite us because we have become fixated on or overwhelmed by the mundane.

Longevity is very important for the entire workforce. Ideally, your organization's turnover rate should be less than 10% (Applauz). A high turnover rate can not only burn through your labor budget because of high training and onboarding costs, but it also can destroy your culture.

So how do you ensure your own longevity and that of your workforce? You must find a way to keep yourself engaged, and then engage and inspire your team. Your organization's employee engagement level is paramount to the health of the entire organization. This is why companies spend thousands—sometimes millions—of dollars hiring management consulting or organizational development firms to measure employee engagement and create action plans.

So how do you remain engaged and help your team to do the same?

The best way to get over the doldrums is to rediscover what excites you. It's likely at the intersection of your gifts, your experiences and your passion. It may be creating a new system or a new spreadsheet. It may be marketing and networking with professionals. It could be teaching others or team building. Whatever it is, write it into your schedule for the week—ideally in the time slot after lunch.

The time management book *Eat That Frog* gives expert advice to make your day the most productive. Productivity starts with doing the toughest, most disliked task of your day first. Wipe it off the to-do list, feel that sense of accomplishment, and then move on. Once the hardest thing is completed first, everything else seems easy!

So schedule that thing you love to do right after lunch. This is the time when most of us get lazy and unproductive, waiting for 5:00 o'clock. Knowing that you're looking forward to your fun project will keep you motivated. Your team will notice, and that motivation will be contagious! Encourage them to schedule their days in a similar way. Let them use their after-lunch time slot for projects they find energizing, rather than scheduling a meeting.

You'll also want to check your mindset daily and remind yourself why you were excited about this job to begin with. Remember that something as basic as work is scriptural. Even when we get to heaven, we won't just be floating around on clouds; there will be work for us to do! Just like Adam was given work to do in the Garden of Eden.

God created work, and he is working in our lives every day. You are his workmanship (Ephesians 2:10), and he won't leave you unfinished. Jesus, too, worked—first with his hands as a carpenter (or as a stone mason, as some historians believe), and then in ministry. And Jesus continues to work on your behalf, preparing a place for you.

Reflect

When was the last time you thanked God for your job?

_____

_____

_____

_____

_____

_____

_____

What aspects of your job are blessings?

_____

_____

_____

_____

_____

_____

_____

What are you passionate about? What are you gifted at doing? How might these intersect at work?

_____

_____

_____

_____

_____

_____

_____

What parts of your job do you love doing? Which parts of your job uniquely demonstrate your abilities?

_____

_____

_____

_____

_____

_____

_____

What are you going to add to your schedule that you enjoy?

_____

_____

_____

_____

_____

_____

_____

_____

Write out a prayer thanking God for your blessings and for the work he's carrying out in your life. Ask God to open your mind to what he wants you to focus on this week and this month.

_____

_____

_____

_____

_____

_____

_____

DAY 2

Flattery Gets You Nowhere,
Be Authentic & Intentional

"Now the purpose of the commandment is love from a pure heart, from a good conscience, and from sincere faith, from which some, having strayed, have turned aside to idle talk..."

1 Timothy 1:5-6 (NKJV)

Put more simply: Be sincere in your love for others, with pure intentions. Use words that are thoughtful and mean something!

Every good parent wants to encourage their child. We tell them, "I'm proud of you," or "You're so smart." But if a parent can tie that compliment to a specific moment when the child exhibited a great skill or virtue, self-esteem is created instead of egotism.

"Amy, you showed how trustworthy you are by how you cared for your pet."

"Caleb, I was so proud of how hard you studied to get that grade."

"You did a fabulous job of organizing your room and making it pretty."

These are just some examples of parent-to-child encouragement. The same is true—and equally important—in the workplace.

Have you ever had a supervisor say things to you like, "Great job!" or "Thanks for all you do," or simply… "You rock!" Maybe you've found yourself saying those words as well. There's nothing wrong with a spirited compliment or knuckle bump, but if that's as deep as you ever get with your show of appreciation, your team will never grow to be vested and committed.

People have to feel valued to dig their heels into your business. Generic, idle words show team members you're "nice." But some may assume you're just trying to check the "encouraging manager" box for your own good—whether that's to be liked or because it's what you read managers are supposed to do. Your team can read the difference between a generic platitude and a genuine, thoughtful, and tailored compliment.

The basic core need of every human being is to be known. People need to be truly seen.

"Nice" bosses can keep people on the bus for a time. But how do you know if they're even in the right seat if you don't know that person's gifts, talents, and experiences? When a person is acknowledged for what they uniquely contribute to the team, they know they're valued. They feel known and seen as the individual they are—not just another cog in the wheel.

In your mind, you're likely thinking about those shining stars on your team—those individuals who show up every day ready to get the job done! They tackle challenges and make your job easier. It's probably easy to create a concrete list of their personal attributes. You may be thinking right now of all the sincere words you can shower them with to tell them they're valued.

Make a list of those top three individuals and at least one specific moment when they made an impression on you or the company. What was the positive impact of their work?

Hopefully that wasn't too challenging. Look for these opportunities every day. Before you rattle off idle words like, "You're doing a great job,"—STOP. Realize that's not a complete thought. How are you going to finish that sentence? Finish it with a concrete statement that shines a light on their impact as an individual.

Now, the same principle applies when correcting. It's easy to point out and give praise to top performers and to highlight their value. The poor performers make this task more difficult.

Wait… Am I suggesting every single team member should be valued even if they stink at their job? You bet I am! If you want to foster the culture of servant leadership, you must be willing to value every single person—even if you don't like them or they are not working up to the standard.

God created every person with a purpose. He created every person to be his workmanship, with individual gifts and talents, and gives each person unique experiences. Every person has value, and as a true servant leader, you must see them as nothing less. It's your role to bring out the best in them. If they feel routinely criticized or overlooked entirely, it's unlikely they'll be motivated to work hard and make improvements.

Now, this doesn't mean someone who makes bad choices, breaks rules, and slacks off should stay employed. Their employment status has nothing to do with their value. But as their leader while they're under your employment—and maybe even after—it's your job to show them their value.

Here's an example from personal experience: Kara was a caregiver. As the Executive Director of the organization, I was not her direct supervisor. Nonetheless, I make it a point to know the entire staff. I could see that Kara loved people. She was caring and very smart. She could create systems that made jobs more efficient. She was a fabulous multi-tasker. She wanted to advance her career and go to nursing school.

However, she started dating a crazy boyfriend who hung out in the clubs until all hours. She started following his lead and began showing up late looking disheveled, and started taking long breaks. I caught her literally sleeping on the job.

When I called her to my office to write her up and give her corrective action, the conversation started with the obvious: "You can't sleep while you're working." It could've ended there. But it didn't. I followed that by saying, "Kara, I think you're amazing. You're so intelligent. You have big dreams. You think of things that no one else can. I so value you. But you're making some terrible choices! You're throwing away your chances. I know you're young, and you have a new relationship. But if that relationship is causing you to throw away your future, it's not worth it. You're too good for this!"

What could have been a five-minute "write-up" turned into an hour-long conversation. She cried. She knew I was right and she agreed with me. We talked about her future, and I promised to do anything I could to help her (and I meant it). She left the office knowing she made mistakes, but she also knew she was valued and that I was on her side.

I wish I could tell you this was a fairytale ending and Kara turned her life around that day. But she chose not to. I ended up parting ways with Kara, but every conversation ended with encouragement. The day I terminated her, I sent her a handwritten card that said, "You're more than you think you are. I'm praying you will see yourself as God sees you."

I don't know where Kara is today, but I know I did what God wanted. I hope those words of encouragement come back to her when she needs them.

This may seem like a lot of energy to put into a person who likely isn't going to make it in your organization. However, if you don't see the good in them, they'll never see it in themselves. The truth is, no one will perform better than you expect them to. If you expect the worst from someone, that becomes a self-fulfilling prophecy. They won't strive to be more. If you expect great things from people, they're far more likely to aspire to greatness!

Takeaways:
- ✓ Don't flatter—encourage!
- ✓ Get to know your team, even those employees you don't like.
- ✓ No one will ever be better than you expect them to be.

Reflect

Consider how you give your team positive feedback. Do you feel you've been ingenuine? If so, how can you change that to authentic praise?

_____

_____

_____

_____

_____

_____

_____

In what specific ways can you encourage your team without flattering them? How can you tailor your encouragement to each individual? Concentrate on your individual team partners or people with in your sphere of influence.

_____

_____

_____

_____

_____

_____

_____

Who is the biggest "problem-child" on your team? Why?

_____

_____

_____

_____

_____

_____

_____

_____

What God-given value do you see in that person? How can you show them you see their value? How can you try to bring the best out of them?

_____

_____

_____

_____

_____

_____

_____

_____

Close in Prayer:

_____

_____

_____

_____

_____

_____

_____

_____

_____

_____

_____

_____

_____

_____

_____

_____

_____

_____

_____

_____

_____

_____

_____

_____

_____

_____

_____

DAY 3

Unify Your Team

"Now I plead with you, brethren, by the name of our Lord Jesus Christ, that you all speak the same thing, and that there be no divisions among you, but that you be perfectly joined together in the same mind and in the same judgment."

1 Corinthians 1:10 (NKJV)

The Bible has a lot to say about unity, especially if you examine the early church. Over and over again, the term "one accord" is used to describe the first believers in Christ. When the Holy Spirit came upon them, they were all of one accord, in one place. All who believed were together and had all things in common. And because of this, they sparked a revolution that changed the world. They were all working together for one cause, one purpose, one mission—to tell people the truth about Jesus.

Webster defines unity as the state of being "joined as a whole." However, if you ask Google what unity is, you'll get a more interesting answer: "Absence of diversity, unvaried or uniform character. Oneness of mind and feeling." I agree with the latter half of Google's definition, but disagree that unity means you can't also have diversity. Unity does not, and should never, devalue individualism. Unity does not stand in the way of valuing the individual characteristics of each member within a group. However, it does mean that each individual operates in like-mindedness with one another, using their diverse talents, expertise, and personality traits toward the common goal.

No two people are alike. Every person has a unique formula of values, strengths, motivations, and abilities. To remove or silence the characteristics and personalities that are God-given is to silence your most valuable resource and stifle your company's growth. A company is nothing more than a group of people who joined together to achieve a common goal. We can achieve those goals when we utilize the strengths of each individual. But to do this, you have to know the strengths of every single person on your team. Being known is a fundamental need of all humans.

For unity to be achieved, the leader has to communicate the group's common goal over and over again until the entire team understands, can communicate that goal, and pursues that goal through their actions. This is authentic belief in the cause. But it also indicates that everyone understands their individual purpose in achieving the goal. They know how their role and job description contribute uniquely to the goal, but the mission is the same. As a servant leader, your job is to intimately know the values, strengths, and abilities of each team member. Then, you'll know how to inspire them individually to accomplish organizational objectives.

During day-to-day operations, there will always be short-term goals that need to be achieved: increase sales, lower costs, reduce workman's comp, etc. However, the overarching goal must be found in the company's mission statement. That mission statement has to be open-ended and leave room for self-expression as it encompasses an ideal. It should motivate the people within the company to feel they're serving something bigger than themselves and that their work matters.

When Peter was called to bring the good news to the Gentiles, he faced opposition. Some people didn't understand the mission. The Jewish people couldn't understand that the truth of Jesus wasn't contained to the Jewish people. Yet, the apostles were still being sent to the Gentiles. Peter was able to restate the mission several times to the team. Paul was a huge supporter, and most of his writing to the Romans explained this mission. Jesus had given them the mission statement for their work before he left the earth: "Go into all the world and preach the gospel to every creature." Now, THAT is a mission statement!

The apostles had a huge job to do. There was a lot of work to be done, and God himself gave them their marching orders, but he did this little by little. Paul, Simon, Peter, Ananias— they were all given different tasks to achieve, but every task aligned with the mission. The mission was clear: "Go and tell the whole world" about what Jesus did!

Here are some company mission statements that you may have heard:

Nike: To bring inspiration and innovation to every athlete in the world.

Starbucks: To inspire and nurture the human spirit—one person, one cup, and one neighborhood at a time.

Coca-Cola: To refresh the world and make a difference.

All of these mission statements leave wiggle room for the individual to find their own place in the company. Whether someone is selling the product, marketing the product, or manufacturing the product, they can feel confident about impacting the world in a positive way.

As a servant leader and manager, you hold people accountable for their role in achieving the mission. There's a connection between an employee's attitude at work and the impact they have on the mission. A foul attitude or mundane work ethic will not "inspire," "nurture," or "refresh." The more passionate employees are about their place in the overall mission, the greater their awareness and care for the bottom line. The servant leader's job is to help the team understand that if the company's financial goals aren't met, the company will cease to exist and can no longer achieve its positive purpose and mission.

Did you catch that? Yes, you *can* and *should* share financial data with your front-line associates! Why do we guard that information like a treasure map? Most assuredly, if it were a treasure map, you'd want everyone swinging a shovel and digging in the right spot. So to show your employees you want and value their full participation in the company's success, the least you can do is share operations, budget, and financial information. When your employees believe leadership trusts and respects them as members of one team working toward the same goal, they're more likely to be invested in the mission, and therefore more willing to dedicate time and energy toward its success.

It's important to point out, not all team members are going to understand. Even the best leaders won't succeed at inspiring everyone. Dissension and arguing within the team will cause people to doubt the mission. I do believe you should try again and again, but once a person is a detriment to the culture you're creating, you'll need to prayerfully remove them. We'll talk more about this later, but remember: A little leaven will leaven the entire lump (Galatians 5:9). And a little fire kindles the entire forest (James 3:5). You have to remove cancer before it affects the whole body.

Take Away:

✓ Every member of the company must feel inspired to bring their unique approach to fulfilling the mission.

✓ As a servant leader, get to know each person's strength and passion. Help them discover how to use it to achieve something bigger than themselves!

✓ The goal and mission need to be revered, referenced, and reiterated often. Celebrate when someone does something that personifies the mission statement!

Reflect

What inspires you about your company's or organization's mission statement?

_____

_____

_____

_____

_____

_____

_____

Who on your team do you need to get to know better?

_____

_____

_____

_____

_____

_____

_____

Have you squashed a team member's passion because you didn't value their unique way of doing things?

_____

_____

_____

_____

_____

_____

_____

How can you incorporate the mission statement into everyday meetings? How will this bring unity?

_____

_____

_____

_____

_____

_____

_____

_____

Close in Prayer:

_____

_____

_____

_____

_____

_____

_____

_____

_____

_____

_____

_____

_____

_____

_____

_____

_____

_____

_____

_____

_____

_____

_____

_____

DAY 4

Build Trust

In Steven Covey's book *The Speed of Trust*, he remarks that a lack of trust causes increased expense and wasted time. The example he uses to illustrate this is airline travel prior to 9/11. Before that tragic day, airline travel was relatively easy. But since the tragedies of 9/11, we all lost some trust in airline travel. To add security and compensate for the lost trust, additional measures were implemented that cost travelers more money and time.

Whereas you used to be able to arrive at the airport an hour before departure—and your loved ones could accompany you right up to the gate—now there are long security lines to get through. You're recommended to arrive at the airport at least two hours before your departure. The extra security measures also cost money, which you see reflected in the price of your airline ticket. So today, there's nothing convenient about traveling because we lost trust.

Now imagine what lack of trust can do within your family structure, your volunteer organization, or the company you lead. When you trust someone's words and actions, you're much more likely to work efficiently, honestly, and without hesitation. If your team were to question your motives, they might pause before acting on your requests. They may even push back, ask others to weigh in, complete the request begrudgingly, or disregard your instructions entirely.

The greatest way to build trust with your associates is to give it. This requires you to expect the best out of them. If you expect someone to let you down or to fail, they're more likely to do just that. This approach may sound risky, but people will never perform their best or work their hardest in a culture where they're not trusted. Lack of trust in your team will force you into a position of micromanaging, and that never brings a company to the next level.

Micromanagers tend to believe they're the only one capable of doing anything right or on time. Even if you don't feel that way, that's the message micromanaging sends. Instead, try freely giving trust. Trust the assignment will get done. Trust that people are telling you the truth. Trust that your associates have the right motivations and intentions.

In Romans chapter 12, Paul tells us to be of the same mind toward one another and not to be wise in our own opinion. That speaks to me. It tells me I'm not necessarily smarter or wiser than anyone on my team simply because I'm the leader. Remember, you've been placed in a leadership position by God, not to do everything yourself, but to inspire, guide, and serve those who serve. Your number one job is to serve the team you lead so they can do their best work—then trust that they'll do it.

Having said this, as a servant leader, there are ways you can jump in and help your team accomplish their work without micromanaging. In my career, I've worked with people of diverse abilities and aptitudes. I've led highly qualified people along with those who struggled to keep up.

In my organization, the nursing departments fall under my leadership. Each nursing department is led by a Director of Nursing who reports to me. Most nurses tend to be right-brained, which makes them loving, caring individuals with a great bedside manner. A personality inclined toward relationship-building and communication normally doesn't thrive in the world of finance or budget talks. But for that role, which is more important?

I've come to understand that no one is good at everything. In this particular instance, I know I have to help these individuals with budget matters, and that they may never fully grasp a P&L spreadsheet. And they don't have to! The best way I can serve my Directors of Nursing is by giving them a spend-down sheet, helping them order supplies, and even taking over their invoicing. By doing that, it frees them up to succeed in their most important task, which is caring for patients and residents.

The greatest compliment I ever received was in an email that said, "Most bosses would rather watch you fail than help you succeed. Thank you for helping me." Every single person has weak spots. And as leaders, we want to teach and help everyone reach their full potential. That's our job! But we also have to realize that if someone needs help in one area, they can still be a valuable and essential part of the team if the most important parts of their job get done.

We can apply Paul's instruction to the Galatians in our workplace. He instructed them to *"Help carry each other's burdens."* There may be mundane tasks your high-performing teammates struggle to accomplish. It may be that they're not naturally gifted in that area, or that certain mundane tasks cause them to lose focus or passion for the most important facets of their job.

Using myself as an example, I'm not detail-oriented. I see the big picture. I hate the minutia of details and can get lost trying to see through the weeds if I'm forced to use a fine-tooth comb. I do try. And I've gotten better, but attention to detail will never be my strength. I've learned to have my associates proofread for me. I've learned to ask, "What am I missing? Am I not seeing something?" I have many strengths, but I can't be good at everything. Neither can you. Neither can your team. We need each other.

Giving trust to build trust also comes into play when taking corrective action with your employees. As we talked about prior, starting a difficult conversation with an authentic attitude, believing the other person has a good heart with good intentions, will dramatically change the tone of that conversation. It will avoid defensiveness from the beginning and slowly create a culture of trust because you're approaching the conversation on the same team.

James 3:17 tells us, *"Wisdom is pure, peaceful, gentle and willing to yield with no partiality."* As a leader of a business, organization, or even a family, this is a cornerstone verse for building trust through open-minded, deep conversation—even if it's not comfortable. However, the more practice you have, the easier these conversations will flow.

As a manager or leader, you likely deal with complaints from customers. Unfortunately, that's a big part of leading. Very often, I've had customers tell me stories of how my employee behaved or spoke inappropriately. Sometimes those complaints are valid, and sometimes they're not. There are two sides (or even three) to every story. As the leader, it's your job to listen to the complaint, do what you can to right the situation, and then talk to your associate. This may happen every day in your industry. Every single time I have one of those associate conversations, I start by believing the associate was acting with pure intentions. Always assume noble intent. I would rather err on the side of grace—every single time!

The conversation may start like this: "Sally, I know you're very passionate about your work and you like to do everything with excellence. I got a call from a customer that I want to run by you to find out what happened." This tells "Sally" that I see her, I value her beyond her job duties, and we're on the same team. In the course of the conversation, she may admit a mistake, or she may think she did everything right. But she's less likely to try to cover her tracks or lie to protect herself because I started the conversation by making her feel protected. Once you have honesty about mistakes, you're riding at the speed of trust!

Now, I'm not naïve, nor do I think every associate is a good one for your team. Yes, there are times you must write corrective actions, a performance plan, or simply let them go elsewhere for employment. That's business, and when it needs to be done, as a leader you must do it. However, you can even approach a termination in a way that serves your associate. Servant leadership doesn't mean allowing sub-par performance, but it does mean that as the leader, every single action you take is motivated by service. Your actions should be motivated by helping the other person grow and become a better version of themselves.

Such a termination conversation can start much the same way. "Sally, I want you to know how much I value you. I see the potential for great things in your future. However, we've lost customers because of the way you speak with people. I know that was not your intention, but I must let you go because your actions haven't changed after our past conversations on this subject." I would likely make the conversation a bit longer, help counsel her on things she should work on for her future, and wish her well.

As hard as this is, Psalm 15:2 tells us to speak the truth from the heart. The whole truth. Not just the good. Not just the bad. The whole truth from the heart, which means from a place of compassion and empathy.

Proverbs 20:28 says, *"Love and faithfulness keeps a king safe. Through love his throne is secure."* If you lead with faithfulness and love, trust will thrive!

Reflect

Are you helping people succeed or watching them fail?

_____

_____

_____

_____

_____

_____

_____

What are some tangible ways you can show your trust?

_____

_____

_____

_____

_____

_____

_____

Do you allow your team to see your vulnerabilities? If not, why?

_____

_____

_____

_____

_____

_____

_____

_____

_____

How can showing your own vulnerabilities build trust?

_____

_____

_____

_____

_____

_____

_____

When you hear a complaint about someone, what's your initial reaction and thought? Do you believe the complaint?

_____

_____

_____

_____

_____

_____

_____

What would it take for you to assume noble intent? What's keeping you from seeing your associates this way?

_____

_____

_____

_____

_____

_____

_____

_____

Who do you need to have a difficult conversation with regarding performance? Pray about it, and then write out what God tells you as you ask Him to give you the words and wisdom for the conversation.

_____

_____

_____

_____

_____

_____

_____

_____

Close in Prayer:

_____

_____

_____

_____

_____

_____

_____

_____

_____

_____

_____

_____

_____

_____

_____

_____

_____

_____

_____

_____

_____

_____

_____

_____

_____

_____

DAY 5

Pass It On

Teaching. Training. Inspiring. Call it whatever you like, but a large part of leading is passing on our knowledge to others. That knowledge covers everything—from performing job functions to understanding the mission, meeting goals, and mentoring others. Remember that as a leader, you have an opportunity to teach more than just job skills; you can also pass on life skills and the wisdom God has blessed you with from your own experiences. Every single thing you've endured in this life, God wants to redeem. And that's exactly what he does when you share your experiences and wisdom with others.

In Luke 22:31-34 we read Jesus telling Peter, "Simon, Simon, behold, Satan demanded to have you, that he might sift you like wheat, but I have prayed for you that your faith may not fail. And when you have turned again, strengthen your brothers." Jesus knows Peter is going to face fear of persecution and ridicule, that he'll deny him three times and experience guilt and shame. But Jesus is preparing Peter to find his faith again after hardship, and to use his experiences to help others, rather than to deny them, downplay them, or shy away from their reality. He is setting Peter up to be the leader of the church. And true leaders take accountability for their actions and draw lessons from their mistakes. They use hard lessons learned to teach and encourage others under their care.

We see in the gospels that Jesus was a hands-on teacher. He knew his time on earth was limited, yet he didn't write a manual for his disciples. He didn't give them step-by-step instructions. Jesus' training model was to invite disciples to follow him, and then he worked. He preached, answered tough questions, healed people, drove out demons, fed people, and even raised people from death. His disciples watched him and listened to every word. Then Jesus told his disciples to go out and do as he had done.

You see, Jesus came to Earth with a very specific job to do. He was sent here to die as a sacrifice for all of mankind and to be raised from the dead so we may never have to fear death and separation from God. But first, his job was to show the love of God to the entire world. He chose to do that through leadership and management. Jesus could've chosen to personally meet every single person on the planet and introduce himself. But that's not what he did. He chose to pour himself into twelve close friends and teach them. Then, in Luke Chapter 9, Jesus gives his disciples all authority and power. He sends them out to perform miracles and teach others what they had learned from Jesus, so the message would keep spreading. He told them the goal and trusted they would get the job done.

When the disciples returned after their missions to reconvene, I can just picture their excitement! How they must've sat with Jesus and told him (and each other) everything that happened on their journeys—a lively debriefing, if you will. I'm sure they were excited to share with Jesus all the details of their project. Maybe they were proud to report certain events, and uncertain about how they handled others. I imagine they would've been interested to hear how Jesus would've handled situations they encountered and looked forward to Jesus' approval. I encourage you to pause and read Luke Chapter 9 for yourself.

Of course, training and empowering your staff is important. However, there is something very thought-provoking that happens in Luke Chapter 9:37-43. In this passage, the disciples had tried to heal a boy possessed by a demon, but they were unsuccessful. They did everything they were taught but were unable to heal this boy on their own. So Jesus went and healed the boy himself.

This tells us something very important about leadership. First, there will be issues that at times your staff won't be able to handle. As the leader, it'll be your responsibility to step in and take care of it yourself or on their behalf. Knowing what you have to do yourself and what you can delegate is an important skill to master as a leader. Secondly, this shows us that at times we can't depend on anyone other than Jesus for our healing. We can't depend on our friends' prayers or our pastor's abilities. We have to go straight to Jesus on our own behalf.

Giving your team time, attention, and grace to your team to share the successes and failures of a project with you is an important part of leading by example and letting your team learn by doing. When you give them the authority to carry out the mission as they see fit, they'll be more inclined to own the successes and the failures. They'll grow and lead others in the authentic wisdom you allowed them to glean. But ultimately, as the leader who delegated and empowered your team, it's up to you to own the outcomes and stand by your team in the decisions they made.

Reflect

Have you ever given all authority and power to someone else to get a job done?

_____

_____

_____

_____

_____

_____

_____

Were they successful? Or why did they fail? Why?

_____

_____

_____

_____

_____

_____

_____

What wisdom and skills do you possess that God wants you to pass on to others?

_____

_____

_____

_____

_____

_____

_____

_____

Who does God want you to pour your wisdom into today?

_____

_____

_____

_____

_____

_____

_____

Close in Prayer:

_____

_____

_____

_____

_____

_____

_____

_____

_____

_____

_____

_____

_____

_____

_____

_____

_____

_____

_____

_____

_____

_____

_____

_____

_____

_____

_____

DAY 6

Turn Whine into Wine

While trying to complete this book over the last several weeks, I've just felt stuck. I'm tired of thinking about it. I'm out of original thoughts. I'm out of words to say, and I'm out of revelations to share.

I've lost sleep, been riddled with anxiety, and have been feeling like a failure. I've been questioning why God even started this process, and doubted I'd be able to complete it. I have zero creativity and no energy to muster it. It's all gone.

Can you relate? Maybe you have no more sales leads. You have no desire to struggle through another staffing schedule. You're fresh out of winning ideas. You can't figure out how to make budget. You lost your passion and question why you're even in this position. You're tired of being the leader. You lack the motivation to hold one more meeting and don't think you have anything useful to say. It's all gone.

But as the leader, you plaster on a smile. You know you can't let your anxiety surface or it could trickle through your team. If they feel your negative energy, they may begin to doubt the mission, and their performance could suffer. The weight of this responsibility causes even more stress for you. You wonder, "Am I just an actor playing a part I'm not cut out for?" These self-doubting moments can derail you.

I was reminded a few days ago about a similar situation in the Bible. Remember when Jesus went to the wedding celebration? In those days, parties and weddings would last for a week. Somehow, the father of the bride failed to order enough wine. But this set the stage for Jesus' first miracle.

John 2 says, "Jesus and his disciples had also been invited to the wedding. When the wine was gone…" When the wine was gone. Gone, empty, all used up, depleted, and no liquor store in sight!

But Jesus is God, right? He's omniscient. He knew before the party that the wine would run out. He could have planned ahead and brought some with him. Another option could have been,

106

when he saw the wine getting low, he could have multiplied it. After all, he does that with the loaves of bread and the fish later on. But not this time.

But Jesus waited until it was gone. Why do you think he chose to wait?

Jesus' choice to wait created a need. He waited until the wine ran out completely, others realized, and his mother asked him to intervene, thereby ensuring people would witness a miracle—an experience they'd have to believe was supernatural. He waited for the wine to be gone so that there was no human intervention. This miracle was all God and there could be no human explanation other than Jesus.

God does his best work when we're in a state of lack. Do you remember what the wedding guests said about the wine Jesus made? John 2:10 records the guests saying, "Everyone brings out the good wine first and then the cheaper wine… But you have saved the best until now!"

When you can't solve your own problems or fix the mess, that's exactly when God will bring out the best. Go to your Heavenly Father in prayer, and ask him to step in and help. Place your faith in him, just like Mary did when she knew Jesus could remedy the wedding situation and save the host couple from embarrassment in front of their guests. When God responds and you find the solution, comfort, energy, or creativity you were lacking, you'll know it wasn't from you—it was all Him.

So as I woke up this morning feeling empty with the heavy weight of failure on my chest, I went to God in prayer for this book. I had nothing to offer and prayed for God to give me creativity and a desire to find the words for these pages.

Today, around lunchtime, the publisher started texting me about a timeline for completion. Those messages brought that fear of failure to me. He asked me to start creating the illustrations. Suddenly, that simple question sparked a different side of creativity and inspired me. And thus, a few hours later this chapter was complete.

In 12 hours, God took me from wanting to give up to excitement and passion to charge forward. You are just a moment away from God. You don't have to give up. Give it to him! He is about to create the *BEST* now!

Reflect

In what area of your life do you feel "all gone," dried up, depleted?

_____

_____

_____

_____

_____

_____

_____

What feelings or thoughts are you hiding?

_____

_____

_____

_____

_____

_____

_____

Where do you feel weak?

_____

_____

_____

_____

_____

_____

_____

_____

_____

What do you need God to do with his miracle power? Make this your closing prayer today.

_____

_____

_____

_____

_____

_____

_____

_____

DAY 7

Only You....

"Let him deny himself and take up his cross daily and follow me."
Luke 9:23 (ESV)

What is your cross?

I've always seen my cross as my burdens—as the personal weakness I struggle against. My cross is the weight of my responsibilities. The weight of my sin. It's the heavy load of taking care of all the things placed in my care. It paints a picture in my mind of crawling up a muddy hill, tattered and dirty, as I fight to muster strength and feel all too weak. I thought this was the picture of *my cross.* But I was wrong! At least partly.

In Matthew 11:28-30, Jesus was very clear that his yoke is easy and his burdens are light. We're told to lay our burdens at his feet. All throughout the Bible, we're told to be anxious for nothing and to resist fear. So when Jesus told us to pick up our cross every single day, he didn't mean for us to become overwhelmed by the weight of our problems, pressures, and responsibilities. So what did he mean? Let's look at what the cross was to Jesus.

The cross was Jesus' destiny. It was his entire purpose for walking this planet. Without the cross, his purpose never would have been completed. The cross is where he bore the sins of all humanity. The cross restored perfect harmony between God and mankind. The cross, stained with blood, was God's plan of redemption for humanity, and Jesus' purpose was to fulfill it.

So, I ask again, what is *your* cross? Your cross is the purpose for which you were created. You may have dreams and ambitions but are those goals in alignment with His destiny for your life? Instead of walking your own path, in your own strength, choose the destiny you've been created for, the work no one else can accomplish. God created you *on* purpose and *for* a purpose! It's your choice, each day, to lay down what you want, and to instead walk in the steps of God's purpose for your life.

Now if finding your life's purpose and living it out seems like a daunting quest, don't worry. Most of us don't yet know our God-given purpose. God doesn't usually show us the completed puzzle, but he'll help you find one piece at a time, and gradually the picture becomes clear. Just take on today, for tomorrow will have worries of its own (Matthew 6:34). Follow him today. Walk through the doors he opens; speak the words he gives you. Just do the next right thing.

To illustrate, I want to give you an example from my own life. My first job in healthcare leadership was miserable for the first two years. The company was broken. The staff were operating like a herd of cats. Every day, I was met at the door with disgruntled, screaming residents like an angry mob with pitchforks: "Last night's dinner was inedible."

"The entertainment never showed."

"The staff lost my laundry."

"The air conditioning was too cold."

You get the idea. I dreaded going to work and would often cry when I left. I could have quit. I had other options. I wasn't happy, but I knew God had placed me in this position. I knew this was part of my purpose because, when I took this position, I believed it was my destiny. I prayed through the process of getting hired, asking God to close any door not intended for me. When I signed my contract, I was committed and had peace with that decision. But, here I was, months into the position, feeling overwhelmed and defeated. Did that mean I wasn't walking in my calling? Absolutely not! God never told us life would be easy. Actually, he told us the opposite. He said "we will have tribulation".

I muscled through, and I'm so glad I did. Around year three, the culture turned. Yes, it took that long and if I would've quit, I never would've experienced the joy and success of seeing the business thrive. I would've missed all the lessons I learned in those first two years and would have had to repeat it someplace else. God kept me there until it was time to move on, twelve years later. And when that time came, *he* opened the doors. I didn't need to take a battering ram to plow open the gate. It happened in his timing, in his way.

Even Jesus had his moment when he didn't like the purpose he was created for. He was so upset that the Bible tells he was sweating drops of blood when he uttered the most powerful words any of us could repeat. "Father, if it is your will, take this cup away from me; nevertheless not my will, but yours, be done." (Luke 22:42) God doesn't ask us to hide our emotions from him. When you're in an intimate relationship with someone, you can speak plainly with them. So it's acceptable to tell God that you're not enjoying the ride right now, as long as you're willing to accept his will for you. It may sound something like this: "Father, I am tired, frustrated, and unhappy. Nevertheless, I'm going to work. I am going to do this job today and I know you'll open the proper doors for me at the proper time. Let your will be done in my life."

I'm once again reminded of Galatians 6:2, where we're instructed to "bear one another's burdens." As a servant leader, that's part of your daily cross. It may not be your ultimate cross, but that's the cross you pick up daily in your God-given position of leadership. You help others carry their burdens. The people you lead, the people you love, the people within your sphere of influence are purposefully placed there. Only you have your unique position of leadership within their lives to help them to bear their burdens. For such a time as this, you have been placed right where you are to serve others as a way of serving God!

So, I ask again… What is your cross?

Reflect

Do you know that you are placed in your position by God?

_____

_____

_____

_____

_____

_____

_____

Why do you think he did that? Why are you in this unique place?

_____

_____

_____

_____

_____

_____

_____

Are you willing to wait on His timing and if so, how does that affect how you face "your cross" everyday?

_____

_____

_____

_____

_____

_____

_____

_____

Close in Prayer:

Write out your prayer that God will show you your purpose. Ask him to show you your next right step. Pray that he would shape your desires and dreams to align with his will for your life. Then give him time to respond. Make sure you journal any picture he brings to your mind and words he speaks to your heart.

_____

_____

_____

_____

_____

_____

_____

_____

_____

_____

_____

_____

_____

_____

_____

_____

_____

_____

_____

_____

_____

_____

_____

Conclusion:

Your mission

Why are you alive today? Wow. That's a tough question! To pay bills? To take care of your family? To make sure the house doesn't fall apart? To go to work? These are all the things that you are doing, but it is not why you are here.

Now, what if I were to ask, why is your company or organization here today? That's likely an easy question. You can rattle off the purpose and mission plainly.

Aflac's mission statement: "To combine aggressive strategic marketing with quality products and services at competitive prices to provide the best insurance value for customers."

Chick-fil-A: To be America's best quick-service restaurant at winning and keeping customers.

Walmart: "Be the destination for customers to save money, no matter how they want to shop."

We discussed mission statements a few days ago as to how they serve and direct a company. A mission statement defines the core reason for existence while outlining purpose. It is a strong string of words that provides direction and purpose. Imagine if you had a strong string of words to define your purpose—an intentional statement that sums up why you exist. Do you think God had a mission statement in mind when He created you? I do!

The things we do every day are important. It's not just about collecting our paycheck or filling our time. The work you do is God's work for you. Writing a mission statement is meant to give you clarity as you partner with your Creator to fulfill your purpose.

A mission statement may change over time, but usually it is an overarching declarative statement that transcends job titles, family roles, or location. LinkedIn has one of the greatest mission statements to easily understand. LinkedIn's mission is "to connect the world's professionals to make them more productive and successful." For a person that innately connects people together to bring out the best partnerships, that could be their personal mission statement.

You can know more about God's purpose for you when you identify common denominators throughout different chapters of your life. Your purpose is not tied to a job or a position in life.

Your work may be the conduit for you to live out your purpose, but it is not the purpose. To better understand God's purpose for you, let's look at how you are unique.

What is that thing you innately do, or maybe something that you are always drawn to? You can't help yourself because this is at the core of your identity. Some examples: children, animals, people in need, making and sharing money, cooking, creating things.

What ways has God uniquely designed you? Here are some words that may resonate with you. Circle them or create your own: creative, empathetic, wise, teacher, charitable, handy, funny, hopeful, energetic, inspirational, passionate, calm, trusting, integrity, hopeful, expressive, organized, nurturer, justice, leader, trustworthy, strong.

What are you passionate about, or what is an area of need that breaks your heart because you are so sensitive in that spot? A good example may be prisoners, or single mothers, or orphans.

Those areas of our heart that are particularly sensitive are there for a reason. God gave you that empathy to draw you to serve that need. A personal mission statement created by God is always going to involve other people. It is never self-serving. For instance, "I exist to make money in order to create a giant car collection" is not why God created you. However, that same person could say, "I exist to inspire others to be a good steward of their finances and resources that God has given them."

Take some time to pray and ask God to show you His creation. What was He thinking when He thought of you? Jot down your thoughts.

Time to write your mission statement!

You can use this to help or come up with other words to begin:

For such a time as this, (Your name) exists to (do what) in order to (result).

Congratulations! Once you are confident in your purpose, your faith grows by miles because you are directed by God. You don't have to live fearful of the future or the unknown. He designed you, and He wants to use you to do what only you can do!

My Personal Mission Statement:

For such a time as this...........

_____

_____

_____

_____

_____

_____

_____

_____

The next step is to take those words, repeat them several times a day, and apply them to your servant leadership. No one else is called to serve or to lead the exact way that you have been created to serve and lead. Thank Him for His wonderful creation—*YOU!*